Warren

Investing & Life Lessons On How To Get Rich, Become Successful & Dominate Your Personal Finance From The Greatest Value Investor Of All Time

Copyright

Table of Contents

Introduction

We all want to become rich, attain financial freedom and live a legacy for many generations to come. But how do we become rich? This is one of the things that many people wonder and this book is here to give you some amazing lessons from the world's greatest investor: Warren Buffet. In his yearly reports as well as multiple interviews, he spreads valuable wisdom that can be quite useful in your investing journey. The best thing about his stream of advice is that it is so practical, so sensible and so simply structured that anyone can apply such advice.

This book will give you not only amazing investing lessons but also amazing life skills that make the perfect investor. You will not only learn how to invest best but also learn how to achieve financial freedom by making the best investments.

Chapter 1: Investing-Most Essential Lessons on Investing

Simply put, Warren Buffett did not become perhaps the greatest investor in all of history by being a short-term thinker. Neither did he become one of the industry's most quoted men by holding his tongue and keeping his opinions under a cloak. Warren Buffett's easy-to-understand advice, folksy way of imparting it and utter humility in answering questions once they are asked all combine to make him one of the finest men out there to take advice from. We will start the journey of learning from Warren Buffet by looking at some amazing investing lessons that will make a great difference as you invest.

Lesson 1: The Art Of Stock-Picking

"If you are not willing to throw away the misplaced romanticism in stocks and put in the time and work that stock-picking demands, then the guy on the opposite side of your trades will likely know more than you do"

Here is where we start when it comes to Warren Buffett and his advice on going for stock: it is not a hobby and thus, should not be treated as one. It is important to understand that picking stocks is not like picking up groceries at the store. Here is what Warren Buffett admitted to doing: when he was starting out, he reckons he spent thousands of hours learning about the stock world and the means of maneuvering; today, he reckons he has doubled that tally. Learning the skills required to build substantial investment is vital, as is taking the whole thing seriously. Warren Buffett used to camp at his local library until he had read every investment publication the library could offer. When he was through with them, he re-read them again, and then some more. If that sounds nondescript to you, then you should know the man was only 11 at this time.

The bottom-line is this: if you are not willing to throw away the misplaced romanticism in stocks and put in the time and work that stock-picking demands, then the guy on the opposite side of your trades will likely know more than you do. This often translates to the ultimate underperformance recipe.

Lesson 2: Leave Emotion At The Door When It Comes To Investing

"Emotion only guides you to refusing to admit missteps and mistakes; to hold onto a losing project for far too long rather than simply cut your losses, put your business trench coat on and move forwards."

Mike Tyson once said that it was in his nature, just as it is in every human being in the world, to be given to emotion and act based on it. If anything, life is so much the wealthier for it. However, the glamour of emotion, unfortunately, does not extend to the investment world.

Emotion greatly eats away at investment returns. If you truly are keen at making some costly systematic mistakes, have emotion as your sidekick as you invest. Emotion will likely also bring its close cousins, cognitive bias and ego, along for the ride too, very much at your expense. Here is what emotion makes you do: rather than dig deep and look for evidence that may fight your position (and thus perhaps save you a lot of misery in the future), it wires you to look for only that evidence that supports it. You will only start to seriously ponder about risk when things are already heading south. Now, while this is bad enough in most areas of life, it has the capacity to be very destructive in the investment world.

Emotion only guides you to refusing to admit missteps and mistakes; to hold onto a losing project for far too long rather than simply cut your losses, put your business trench coat on and move forwards.

Emotion is a funny beast in how it works too; rather than have a clear head of what you expect to make and reinvest, it focuses you too much on how you will spend the money you earn from the investment you are making. Is there anything wrong with this? Not necessarily, until you come across Warren Buffett's wise words. He said, *"You do not spend the money you get from investments, you reinvest it again"*.

Besides, the overconfidence and excessive optimism that emotion pins to your belief of your investment abilities is far too dangerous in the investment world. Keep emotion off your workstation.

Lesson 3: "Invest In Familiarity"

If there is one thing that Mr. Buffett stressed on over and over again is the importance of having a flat circle of ultra-competence. Basically, what this points to is investing in an industry that is clearly marked out, a business model that has been carefully drawn out, an investment style that has a sheaf of factual material to back it up etc. Of course, you must continue to learn, thereby making the circle larger. Warren Buffett has 3 mailboxes he keeps on his desk. The labels on them are "in", "out" and "too difficult". Every business has, admittedly, factors that qualify as known, unknown, vital and unimportant. For maximum gains though, Buffett recommends that you invest in a business in which the vital/important factors are known. Why so? According to him, the only reason he will pick something is to be with it for the long haul. He wants to estimate, with a degree of accuracy, how that business will look like in 5 to 10 years.

So what does this mean to you as an investor? Always invest in investments that you are familiar with or at least industries that you know a thing or two about. However, this does not mean that you simply stick to such businesses or investments.

Your goal is to continue learning and improve your knowledge of different kinds of investments therefore, increasing your chances of succeeding in any kind of investment you make.

Lesson 4: Owning Stock Is Owning A Business, Not A Bunch Of Digital Charts

"You need to think of it (owning stock) as something of a partial ownership in the main business body that underlies it"

You cannot afford to look at stock as an over-glorified line on a chart that moves up, at least hopefully, over time. You need to think of it as something of a partial ownership in the main business body that underlies it. Unlike, say, precious stones or collectibles, stocks have intrinsic value attached to them because your very ownership gives you a claim of proportion to the corporation's earnings in the future. How so? In the form of dividends, of course. If the business does well in a stretch of time, the price of the stock will eventually follow suit. Warren Buffett looks at himself, not as an analyst of the market or perhaps an analyst of the macroeconomic sort, but as an analyst of business. It is time you viewed yourself as so.

Chapter 2: Warren Buffett's Stand On Stock Repurchases, Bull Markets, Identifying A Good Company & The Basic Role Of The Market

Warren Buffett & Stock Repurchases

Oftentimes, companies will repurchase shares and this will be at the expense of shareholders. Here is one thing Warren Buffett loves to educate investors on: management often has a knack of repurchasing shares at prices that are bloated. Certainly, if you look at it, it will appear as though the true objective of the management is to increase the share's price in order to increase the option value. Here is something you will find interesting: just like many people, the management may be just as bad at investing. Those 3 letters, CEO, do not make a "Buffett". It will serve you well to remember that.

Here is what Mr. Buffett had to say on the same:

"I have said this before and I will say it again; the intrinsic value of Berkshire by far exceeds that of its book value. If anything, the difference has only grown as the years have passed by. This is the reason why back in the year 2012, we came to the decision to authorize the share repurchase at a hundred and twenty percent (120%) of the book value. By all accounts, this made and still makes tremendous sense. Making purchases at this level does a lot to benefit the shareholders that are continuing seeing as the intrinsic value, per-share, exceeds book value percentage by quite a fair amount. In 2013, we stayed away from buying shares, reason being, stock price did not drop to the 120% base. If by any means it does, we promise aggression."

This is all clear, consistent and concise. Investors and yes, CEOs, will do well to go by Warren Buffet's example.

Warren Buffett And What He Thinks Of Bull Markets

"Bull markets are immense fun, until they cease to be immense fun."

In all sureness, there must be quite a large number of people enjoying the recent rise that has taken place in the market. For these men and women of the investors' world, Buffet speaks out to them like only he is capable of:

"Remember Barton Briggs, the late great? He had this observation: "A bull market very much resembles sex". It is, and feels, at its best just before the climax hits and it all ends."

Is the market feeling pretty good right about now? If it is, remember Barton Briggs. If you didn't know him, then simply understand that Warren Buffett endorses his immortal words. That has to be something in itself, isn't it?

Warren Buffett's Advice On Identifying A Good Company

The essential characteristics list that Warren Buffet has drawn up and looks for when it comes to investments is short, and this is a surprising thing in itself.

What does Warren Buffet want in a company? What exactly is he looking for? Warren Buffet wants a company that is remarkably easy to understand, a business that boasts of an operating history that is consistent; superb prospects where the long haul is concerned.

It doesn't stop there though. The list continues.

Warren Buffet wants a company that identifies itself as competitive, not just by way of its motto but in a deeper sense- it places itself on the map and allows competition to refine its brand and help it operate at the very highest level. Buffet wants a company with financials that are solid: financials marked by lofty margins, a lofty return where equity is concerned and cash flow that is both high and free. He does fancy a company that is prone to growth, but his love for growth isn't as exaggerated as that of those who love to move and operate in the short term. Buffet understands that where companies are concerned, it is very hard for growth to last more than a few years owing to the outsize profits drawing in serious competition.

The Basic Role Of The Market According To Warren Buffett And How To Approach It

Warren Buffet summarized this in one staccato sentence: "The market is there to give service to you, not to act as your informant."

Ben Graham, whom Warren Buffett admired greatly, designed a thought experiment that Buffet would later use extensively. Here it is:

Just imagine that the stock market takes on the form of a single individual; a guy that goes by the name of Mr. Market. Apparently, Mr. Market is 100% willing to as well as able to purchase stock of any kind from you as well as sell any kind of stock to you. Oftentimes, Mr. Market is a rational guy and the prices he tags to his wares are often reasonable but sometimes, emotion tends to overtake him, makes him irrational and results in prices that swing in wild form. When Mr. Market has this rational element going on for him, so that he has no great deals to palm your way, you are free to ignore him (hence, why patience is such an important skill to develop). When he's greedy, you may make your sale to him on premium. When he has fear gnawing at him, you may buy from him at a discount. However, never underestimate him-he's usually approximately right, whichever way things swing.

We cannot talk about investing, how to identify a good market, returns, losses and gains without mentioning tax. This is because if you are not careful, all the returns you make can actually be used to pay taxes then you are left with nothing or something quite minimal. Therefore, we will look at Buffet's valuable advice when it comes to taxes.

Chapter 3: The Taxman-Warren Buffett's Invaluable Advice On The Art Of Tax-Loss Selling

Warren Buffet also has invaluable advice on tax-loss selling that you can benefit greatly from. This strategy of tax loss selling allows the investor to sell off investments that are losing and then follow this up by applying those losses against any gains they may have been subject to during the financial year. Have a look at this example in order to understand this strategy much better

An investor who has sold off investments that produced a gain of 1000 dollars could sell off an investment that has registered losses of 1000 dollars in order to offset that 1000 dollar gain the former investment gained and thus, avoid any taxes on it. Simple stuff, right?

With tax-loss selling, short term losses can be applied directly against gains that are short term as well, with long term losses also applied against gains that are of a long term nature. Once those calculations are done and dusted, the investor may then apply any remaining short or perhaps long-term losses against any short or long-term gains. If at all any losses are still available, un-applied, the

IRS gives the investor the option of using up, up to 3000 dollars worth of them in a bid to reduce the taxable income. Any additional losses may also be carried forward to the future years. This sounds like a superb strategy- and by all means it is but there is a catch.

So that the loss may be applied to offset gains, then the loss must be effectively sold by the close of the tax year. In addition, you, the investor, may not re-purchase the same stock or even a derivative of that stock for a period of 1 month (30 days).

Warren Buffet has also provided some valuable advice on taxes and this is advise that should make any wise investor have a brief pause before hitting the "sell" button on an investment that is losing. In the year 1965, Buffet penned a letter to the investors of the world. This is what he had to say:

"What is an investor really trying to accomplish in this world of investing? Not pay off the least taxes to the taxman, although this is a solid factor that may be in consideration in achieving the end goal. The means and the end must never be confused, and the end is to be able to come away with the heftiest after-tax compound rate".

Warren Buffett did not stop there. He went a step further to issue a warning to investors on the risk of blindly acting based on the investor's distaste for paying taxes.

For every investor, Warren Buffett's statement serves as a reminder of value seeing as it shifts the focus firmly back from selling off a stock with the aim of offsetting a gain to answering this question: has anything at all changed at this company that would prompt the will in me to sell? This is, by all means, a far more vital question to ask yourself when it comes to your losing investments. The answer that you come up with for this question must weigh, by a significant volume, the decision to take up a taxable loss so as to cut down on your overall tax bill.

Thinking In The Long Haul

If you have read on investing, you will know that it is inevitable that the market must pop and drop, then rinse and repeat the same. Even the best of businesses will, on occasion, punish investors at times. However, selling off great companies so that you may cut down on what you owe to the taxman may well jeopardize your investments in future. This is because the bulk of investors have this thing where they tend to steer clear of repurchasing stocks that they may have sold off at losses because they balk at the possibility of repeating the same mistake. As a result, rushing off to sell may well deprive you of future years of phenomenal growth.

In Buffett's eyes, the better solution is to put your focus firmly on the long haul. If at all something has changed fundamentally to the reasons you decided to invest in a company then by all means sell it off and take the loss with heart. However, if nothing else has changed except the share price of the stock, it is wiser to sit tight and avoid hitting the "sell" button.

According to Buffett, people like you are not the only ones looking to reduce the tax bill. Companies have found an ingenious loophole that allows them to reduce a large of amount of income tax. Here is the catch, however: they have to pay you, the investor, so as to keep enjoying that tax break. Now you see how the IRS can actually be your pal? It is alarming the number of investors who have no clue such a phenomenon exists.

Chapter 4: Life Skills That Work For Investors-Buffett's Selection Of Life Skills To Make You A Business Heavyweight

In addition to investment skills that you need as well as some invaluable information on how to choose a good company and how to go about taxation as outlined in the previous chapters, you also need to essential life skills if you are to be the best investor. We will look at these life skills in this chapter.

Life Skill No.1: Patience

Here is one of Buffet's sound bites, "Business and baseball share the biggest difference in that in investments, called strikes are absent". With investing and business as a whole, you may well stand at the plate all season long and have your bat limp by your side if you do not see any pitches that you fancy. However, this may well prove to be quite difficult seeing as the finance systems pushes the need for frequent trading. This is understandable, given that the revenues tend to grow as the volume of transaction grows.

Here is the thing though: truly great investment opportunities are extremely rare. So as to resist that nagging temptation to do your trade in and out in the positional sense, Warren Buffett himself suggests that you pretend that you can only make a total of 20 trades in your entire time on earth. Under this straight jacket, you would have to conduct adequate research and only move forward when you are confident of a trade. The other dimension of patience, as per Warren Buffett, has everything to do with the horizon of time. The right mentality is to get rich slow as opposed to getting there with pace. Stats do not lie: the bulk of wealthy folk, Buffett included, who have managed to keep their wealth and multiply it earned it by sheer consistency and over quite a large time span.

Life Skill No.2: Be Averse To Loss

There are too many investors on Wall Street who measure performance based solely on the returns gained. While that is a sensible and good measure in itself, a better measure would be a risk-adjusted return. Do not strive to generate every last dime of profit, at least in the potential sense; if you do so, you expose yourself to unnecessary and harmful risk. Rather, it is more advisable to make capital preservation one of your leading goals. Here is how this works: by staying focused on this, your natural gravitation will be towards investments that have more upside potential as opposed to more downside potential. This will work just about perfectly in helping your returns.

The other thing is this; by setting your psychology up so that you are always looking for a safety margin, the returns that you get are guaranteed to almost always be adequate, regardless of how things go out in their respective business pipeline. It really is not that much of a necessity to perform extraordinary feats so as to derive an extraordinary result-the key thing is to avoid making the big mistakes and allowing the phenomenon that is compounding enough space and time to work its magic.

Warren Buffett has an interesting way of putting it: "Rule no.1, thou shall not lose money. Rule no.2, refer to rule no.1"

Life Skill No.3: Be Cheap

Knowing what a good company looks like is a great thing in itself. However, simply buying into every good company that you find is reckless; something that the investors' world could punish you deeply for. The key to Buffett's winning strategy is to unearth good companies at superb prices. What is "price" as per Warren Buffett? Price is basically what you shell out and value is simply that which you get in return. When the cards fall in place and value rises so that it towers over price, the net result is what Buffet's own mentor, Mr. Ben Graham, used to refer to as a margin of safety. When your margin of safety can be described as large, this ultimately enables you to be successful even if things do not quite fall in place as you may have expected them to.

Very early on in his investing career, Warren Buffett tried to stick to only good companies that came with great prices. Later on however, perhaps owing to the fact that he had a substantial amount of capital to deploy every passing year in new investment options, he loosened his rigors and started going for great companies at good prices.

Either way, there is a lot of validity in going either way.

Life Skill No.4: Condition Your Brain To Develop The Mental Strength It Takes To Embrace Volatility

"If you buy good companies at good prices and the prices happen to fall, you may bask in the confidence that soon, the markets will realize these companies deserve to be higher priced. In the unlikely event that the market doesn't realize it, then you may simply sit tight and pocket a steady stream of dividends"

Multiple investors make the mistake of confusing volatility with the phenomenon that is risk. However, it clearly is not that. When you are risk averse, it does not equate to avoiding volatility. Case in point; Berkshire Hathaway, Warren Buffett's own company, has had its stock suffer a quotational loss of north of 50% a total of 3 times in its history, a daunting number of times when you think of it. The interesting part is that Warren Buffet has never parted with more than 2% of his gross net worth on any of those positions. Actually, he has never lost more than 2% of his net worth on any position in his entire life as an investor. How did he do this? The man does not diversify, as so many investors tend to do. Indeed, Buffet has this knack of being heavily concentrated in his investments. At one unique point in his investing career, though a little early on, he actually had 75% of his entire net worth in Geico.

Buffett achieved this by purchasing good companies at prices that were equally good and then bulking up his hold of shares when the prices fell. Never fear the often unstable cloak that the market often wears- volatility is actually the investor's best friend. Especially if you embrace the aforementioned life skills that Buffet offers- patience and a lack of emotional gravitation- you will never have as good a friend as volatility. If anything, Warren Buffett argues that a market that is wildly fluctuating will mean that businesses with a solid base will occasionally be available for purchase at prices that are lower than what would be considered normal. Here is what Buffett's mentor said; "Markets are voting machines in the short run but when it comes to the long run, they take on the nature of weighing machines."

Is there any specific advice to investors looking to invest in America? The following chapter will be of great help.

Chapter 5: Living The American Dream-Investing Advice For The Business-Savvy Individual Who Would Like To Invest In America

Lesson 1: The Future Of America

This is as simple as possible: Mr. Warren Buffett is nothing short of Bullish when it comes to America. Here are some of his choice words on the same:

"Charlie and I; we have always considered betting on the ever-elevating prosperity of this great country, to be as close to a thing of surety as is possible. Indeed, give me a soul that has benefitted in the past 237 years or so by betting against this country. If you look at the present condition of the U.S and then hold it parallel to what was the norm in 1776, you will begin to experience a nagging wish to rub your eyes in sheer wonder. The market economy is intense in its dynamism- this magic will keep on working itself and replicating. One thing is for sure, the best days of America are not here yet: they lie ahead."

That is as moving as anything ever gets. Get this; however, his optimism is not just unfounded. Berkshire-Hathaway's buy out of BNSF back in the year of 2009 was, as the man himself lays it down, an "all in wager on the future, at least economically, of the U.S." On a similar platform, he has instructed the one trustee who will manage the money he leaves his wife to pump about 90% of it in a low cost 500 index fund. What about the other 10%? This will go to a short term U.S government bond fund.

Get this, as Warren Buffett sees it, "The best days of America are not here yet: they lie ahead." So if you are holding back, for whatever reason, at going all out and investing in companies in this great country, listen to what Buffet has to say then buckle down and make things happen.

Lesson 2: You Invest, Not In Stocks, But In Businesses

This does not only apply in the U.S, but everywhere else in the world. Take this for instance: supposing you were ready to buy a real business and had the capital for an instant then a friend tells you that there is a gas station up for sale at the sum of 1 million dollars. We all know gas stations often hold the capacity to pump out sizable returns, but would you leap at the opportunity and make the purchase without looking at the necessary information first? The answer would be no, seeing as that is a foolhardy thing to do. You would have to put yourself in a position where you understood things like its revenue and expenses first.

Yet, when it comes to stocks, a lot of investors think they can play the stock market without knowing much about the particular business they are buying. Even more disturbing, they think they can pull it off with consistency. Often, investors are all too consumed with quotations of the market.

Warren Buffett takes a different and unique approach:

"With my 2 small-sized investments (here, he is referring to two properties that he has just bought), I concentrated my thoughts only on what each property would produce, and not on such

27

matters as daily valuation. Take a look at sports: games are often won by players who put their focus on the playing field and not by the squad whose collective pairs of eyes are married to the scoreboard alone. If at all you can enjoy your weekends without paying heed to the stock prices, give this a try when the weekdays come around."

Lesson 3: Keep Your Focus On Per Share Results

Warren Buffett maintains a keen and deliberate focus on per share results. He compares growth in the book value of Berkshire, per share, to how the S&P 500 performs. Buffett went further to explain that his goal was "simply not growing in girth", but "increasing the per-share result consistently".

Here is how he describes his goal and the method he would put in place to achieve his goal:

"There's a tailwind working here, and with this tailwind working for Charlie and I, we hope to bulk up Berkshire's per-share value by (1) improving that basic earning power of our multiple subsidiaries constantly; (2) further bulking up these earnings via acquisitions that are bolt-on; (3) benefiting from that growth that our investees experience; (4) re-buying the shares of Berkshire when they do indeed become available at a discount that is meaningful; (5) making, on occasion, a large acquisition. We will also do our best to maximize the results for you by very rarely, if at all ever, issuing the shares of Berkshire."

Dilution does matter. The company that does grow in earnings in the aggregate form yet reduces them via dilution on a basis that is per-share proves this

29

axiom: a rising tide targets all boats, regardless of who is in them, and sinks them.

Conclusion

Warren Buffet is undoubtedly one of the greatest investors of all time. It is no wonder that he was able to amass such wealth in his life. Therefore, using his amazing life lessons and skills, as outlined in this book, you can definitely become a Warren Buffet in your own way and achieve financial freedom and success that we all yearn for.